Script *for* FINANCES

LIFE-CHANGING WORDS OF FAITH
FOR EVERY DAY

HARRISON HOUSE
Tulsa, Oklahoma

CONTENTS

INTRODUCTION

God's Word is perfectly clear that it is God's will for you to prosper and be successful in this life. Throughout the Bible you can see the expressions of God's will of abundance toward those who loved Him. There are hundreds of examples in the Bible of God supernaturally providing for His people. One of the redemptive names of God is Jehovah Jirah—the God who provides. Many times in the Bible God is referred to as El Shaddai (the God who is more than enough). God never intended for any of His children to be poor or barely getting along. His plan for your life is financial blessing and abundant provision. Just because it is God's will for you to prosper, however, doesn't mean it will happen automatically. You have to believe His promises, reach out in faith, and snatch them for yourself.

Everything we receive from God we receive by faith. A key factor in releasing your faith is the words that come out of your mouth. There is power released into your life when you speak God's Word. It is a vital part of appropriating God's promises and activating spiritual forces that will bring God's promises to manifestation.

Jesus said in Mark 11:23-24 "that whosoever shall say unto this mountain, Be thou removed, and be thou cast into the sea; and shall not doubt in his heart, but shall believe that those things which he *saith* shall come to pass; he shall have whatsoever he *saith*. Therefore I say unto you, What things soever ye desire, when ye pray, believe that ye receive them, and ye shall have them." Speak to the mountain in your life and it will obey you! WOW! Isn't that awesome?

The confessions in this book are faith declarations based on God's Word. I encourage you to speak them daily over your life. No matter what shape you are in financially, God has a plan for your financial blessing. Even if you are in the middle of an overwhelming financial crisis, there is hope, there is help, there is victory in the life-altering power of speaking God's Word. Be faithful to speak His Word. Release your faith as you speak, and say these declarations boldly. Speak with power and authority. Release your faith and lay claim to the prosperity that is rightfully yours. Now start speaking—and get ready to experience God's power in your life!

Start the Day With God

This is the day that the Lord has made, and I will rejoice and be glad in it. My God supplies all my needs according to His riches in glory. It is His will that I prosper and lack nothing. I am the head and not the tail. I am above and not beneath. I am blessed coming in and I am blessed going out. I am blessed on my job; I have God's favor with all those who are in authority over me.

Abraham's blessing is mine. Abundance and prosperity are God's will for my life. I call all of my debts "paid off" and all of my bills "paid on time." Whatever I do succeeds, and I prosper in whatever I put my hand to. I operate and function in the wisdom of God concerning all my financial matters. Men give to me good measure, pressed down and shaken together, and running over. Supernatural money-making ideas come to me. God gives me supernatural insight and understanding on how to make more money and how to manage all of my financial affairs. I have more than enough to meet all of my needs and plenty left over to be a blessing to others.

Scriptures

This is the day which the Lord hath made; we will rejoice and be glad in it.

Psalm 118:24

The Lord shall make thee the head, and not the tail; though shalt be above only, and thou shalt not be beneath.

Deuteronomy 28:13

The Lord shall preserve thy going out and thy coming in from this time forth, and even for evermore.

Psalm 121:8 NIV

Give, and it shall be given unto you; good measure, pressed down, and shaken together, and running over, shall men give into your bosom. For with the same measure that ye mete withal it shall be measured to you again.

Luke 6:38

God Is My Source

My God supplies all my needs according to His riches in glory. It is God's will that I prosper. He is Jehovah Jirah, my provider. Jesus was made poor that I might become rich. I am blessed by the Lord, and if I honor Him, He will honor me. Wealth and riches are in my house. The Lord is my shepherd; He takes care of me. Therefore, I shall not suffer from want or lack anything. I do not fear, I am not troubled or anxious, and I do not worry about my finances.

I know that God takes care of the birds and the flowers, and I am much more important to Him than they are. And since I know that He takes care of them, then for sure I know He will take good care of me. Therefore, I will not worry about where I will get the money I need for the necessities of life such as food, rent, car payments, clothes, or mortgage payments. My job is not my source, my relatives are not my source, and my credit cards are not my source. God is my source of supply, and He will never let me down.

Scriptures

My God shall supply all your need according to his riches in glory by Christ Jesus.

Philippians 4:19

Ye know the grace of our Lord Jesus Christ, that, though he was rich, yet for your sakes he became poor, that ye through his poverty might be rich.

2 Corinthians 8:9

Even the very hairs of your head are all numbered. Fear not therefore; ye are of more value than many sparrows.

Luke 12:7

Humility and the fear of the Lord bring wealth and honor and life.

Proverbs 22:4 NIV

The Tithe

I am a tither! The tithe is the Lord's, and it is a privilege and honor to give Him 10 percent of all my income. When I am obedient to do so, then the windows of heaven are opened to me and they pour out overwhelming blessings of abundance. Because I am a tither, God has promised to rebuke the devourer for my sake. Therefore, the devourer is rebuked in my life. My possessions don't wear out as quickly as they used to. They last much longer than their normal life expectancy. Even my vehicles last longer and run better, and my household appliances work better and longer than normal. Satan's strategies to steal, hinder, or stop my financial blessings are rendered null and void.

As I give my tithe, I honor the Lord and declare that my financial prosperity is independent of the world's system. No matter what the economy does, my finances are blessed. No matter what the stock market does, my finances are blessed. No matter what the interest rates are, my finances are blessed. No matter what the price of gas, God will supply all of my needs. Because I am faithful to honor God, He will honor me. He is faithful to bring abundance and prosperity to me.

Scriptures

Then Jacob made a vow, saying, "If God will be with me, and keep me in this way that I am going, and give me bread to eat and clothing to put on, so that I come back to my father's house in peace, then the Lord shall be my God. And this stone which I have set as a pillar shall be God's house, and of all that You give me I will surely give a tenth to You."

Genesis 28:20-22 NKJV

Bring ye all the tithes into the storehouse, that there may be meat in mine house, and prove me now herewith, saith the Lord of hosts, if I will not open you the windows of heaven, and pour you out a blessing, that there shall not be room enough to receive it. And I will rebuke the devourer for your sakes.

Malachi 3:10,11

I give tithes of all that I possess.

Luke 18:12

My God shall supply all your need according to his riches in glory by Christ Jesus.

Philippians 4:19

Favor

I have favor with God and man. The Lord has blessed me with favor that surrounds my life like a shield. God's favor has crowned my life with joy, peace, and lovingkindness. His favor goes before me and prepares my way. The Lord is gracious, merciful, and kindhearted toward me. He gives me favor in every area of my life. He gives me favor with everyone with whom I interact. I have favor with my family; I have favor with my employer and coworkers: I have favor with anyone I transact business with. Good deals are always coming to me; people are always blessing me with goods, services, and preferential treatment.

God's favor takes me where my own ability and wisdom cannot. God's favor opens doors of opportunity to me on a regular basis. His favor also puts me in the right place at the right time. Because of His favor, things always turn out working to my benefit.

Men give to me good measure, pressed down, shaken together, and running over. Wonderful things are always happening to me, so it's a surety that something good is going to happen to me today.

Scriptures

Thou, Lord, will bless the righteous; with favour wilt thou compass him as with a shield.

Psalm 5:12

A good man obtaineth favour of the Lord; but a man of wicked devices will he condemn.

Proverbs 12:2

The Lord bless thee, and keep thee; the Lord make his faces shine upon thee, and be gracious unto thee; the Lord lift up his countenance upon thee, and give thee peace. And they shall put my name upon the children of Israel; and I will bless them.

Numbers 6:24-27

Bless the Lord, O my soul, and forget not all his benefits: ...Who redeemeth thy life from destruction; who crowneth thee with lovingkindness and tender mercies.

Psalm 103:2,4

Being Led by the Holy Spirit

Jesus sent the Holy Spirit to be my counselor, guide, and partner in all areas of my life. Therefore, I acknowledge Him and receive Him as my financial advisor. He leads, guides, and directs me in every financial decision of my life. I am led by the Holy Spirit in all financial matters. I am keen to hear and quick to obey the Holy Spirit in all areas concerning my finances. I am sensitive to His voice because I walk in the Spirit. I will not fulfill the lust of my flesh by buying things I don't need, and I won't spend money on foolish pursuits.

I will not enter into any financial arrangement or transaction until I have the peace of God in my spirit regarding what I should do. I will not let my flesh or another person pressure me into buying something that I don't have peace about. Whenever I have a financial decision to make, the Holy Spirit gives me clear and distinct direction. The Lord has given me wisdom, insight, and discernment concerning every detail of my financial affairs.

Scriptures

As many are led by the Spirit of God, they are the sons of God.

Romans 8:14

Sojourn in this land, and I will be with thee, and will bless thee; for unto thee, and unto thy seed, I will give all these countries, and I will perform the oath which I sware unto Abraham thy father; And I will make thy seed to multiply as the stars of heaven, and will give unto thy seed all these countries; and in thy seed shall all the nations of the earth be blessed.

Genesis 26:3-5

Blessed is the man that walketh not in the counsel of the ungodly, nor standeth in the way of sinners, nor sitteth in the seat of the scornful. But his delight is in the law of the LORD; and in his law doth he meditate day and night. And he shall be like a tree planted by the rivers of water, that bringeth forth his fruit in his season; his leaf also shall not wither; and whatsoever he doeth shall prosper.

Psalm 1:1-3

Control of My Flesh

I walk in the Spirit; therefore, I will not fulfill the lust of my flesh. I will not let the temptation of jealousy, pride, or envy influence my spending decisions. I am a faithful steward over the money that comes to me. I will not give in to the temptation to lust after material things as things are not my God. I don't care what people think; I am free from the peer pressure of other people. I am in control of my emotions and of my flesh. I will not go into debt for trivial things. I will not charge items on credit cards unless I know that I can pay for them by the end of the month. I am in total and complete control of my spending.

I will not allow my flesh or pressure from others to force me into compromising my decision to be a good steward over my finances. It's easy for me to say no to poor financial decisions. God has promised that if I will seek Him first, then all the things that I need will be added to me. It is easy for me to be patient and steadfast in my faith until I see the manifestation of the things I really need.

Scriptures

Walk in the Spirit, and ye shall not fulfil the lust of the flesh.

Galatians 5:16

Take no thought, saying, What shall we eat? Or What shall we drink? Or, Wherewithal shall we be clothed? ...But seek ye first the kingdom of God, and his righteousness; and all these things shall be added unto you.

Matthew 6:31,33

The simple believes every word, But the prudent considers well his steps.

Proverbs 14:15 NKJV

Teach me knowledge and good judgment, for I believe in your commands.

Psalm 119:66 NIV

God's Mercy

God is good and His mercy endures forever. He is faithful and just to forgive me of my sins and help me to stay on track. God is a good God, and it is His will for me to prosper and to enjoy good things. God is not mad at me; He loves me and He wants to bless me with abundance. No matter how many times I have messed up—even if what I did was really bad—He still loves me. He doesn't condemn me, and He's not disappointed in me. He is cheering me on because He wants me to succeed.

Even when I make stupid mistakes, God still loves me. Even when I fail Him, He still loves me. Even when I miss the mark and slide into sin, He still loves me and is quick to forgive me when I confess my sins. Even when my financial difficulties are the result of my own poor decisions, He still promises to deliver me, restore me, and prosper me. His plan for my life is success and abundance. He will never fail me even when I fail Him. He crowns my life with tender mercies and lovingkindness.

Scriptures

If we confess our sins, he is faithful and just to forgive us our sins, and to cleanse us from all unrighteousness.

1 John 1:9

If my people, which are called by my name, shall humble themselves, and pray, and seek my face, and turn from their wicked ways; then will I hear from heaven, and will forgive their sin, and will heal their land.

2 Chronicles 7:14

Remember, O Lord, thy tender mercies and thy lovingkindness; for they have been ever of old.

Psalm 25:6

For You, Lord, are good, and ready to forgive, And abundant in mercy to all those who call upon You.

Psalm 86:5 NKJV

God's Blessings at Work

I am faithful and diligent to do my job with excellence. I will do my best to honor God by giving my employer my best, and they will be glad they hired me. I will perform my daily tasks at work with a great attitude, with impeccable integrity, and as a workman worthy of his hire.

Because I am faithful, I will abound in blessings. God gives me insight and understanding on how to do my job better. He shows me ways to perform my duties in an exceptional manner and how to work more effectively and efficiently. Because God's favor is on me and I do my job with excellence, I believe my employer will recognize my value and contribution to the organization and will give me raises, bonuses, and promotions as a result. God prospers the company I work for so they can bless me.

God gives me new and creative ideas on how to make money. I do my work as unto the Lord. Whatever I put my hand to prospers. Because I am faithful in what is another man's, and because I am faithful over little things, the Lord will see to it that I am promoted to bigger things.

Scriptures

The labourer is worthy of his hire.

Luke 10:7

Blessings shall come on thee, and overtake thee, if thou shalt hearken unto the voice of the Lord thy God.

Deuteronomy 28:2

Keep the charge of the Lord thy God, to walk in his ways, to keep his statutes, and his commandments, and his judgments, and his testimonies, as it is written in the law of Moses, that thou mayest prosper in all that thou doest and whithersoever thou turnest thyself.

1 Kings 2:3

Well done, good and faithful servant; thou has been faithful over a few things, I will make thee ruler over many things.

Matthew 25:23

When Bad News Comes

I am not shaken when I hear bad news. I will not let a bad report affect my joy or rob me of my peace. I will not let bad news discourage me or cause me to become fearful. God has a plan for me to overcome this financial adversity. This was no surprise to Him. He will make a way where there seems to be no way. I cast all the problems of this situation over on the Lord. I will not let worry, fear, or anxious thoughts trouble me. The Holy Spirit gives me insight, wisdom, and favor to navigate my way through this adversity.

God is my provider, my deliverer, and my strong tower. I have learned to live independent of circumstances. The Holy Spirit gives me clear and specific directions concerning what I should do. Jesus will never leave me or forsake me. Therefore I will not let my heart be troubled. I will trust in God and I will boast in His Word. What the enemy has meant for evil, God will turn it to my good. I will patiently wait and see the salvation of the Lord.

Scriptures

I will even make a way in the wilderness.
Isaiah 43:19

Let not your heart be troubled; ye believe in God, believe also in me.

John 14:1

Let not your heart be troubled, neither let it be afraid.

John 14:27

[The Lord said] I will never leave thee, nor forsake thee.

Hebrews 13:5

Speak to the Mountain of Debt

Jesus said that if I speak to the mountain in my life it will have to obey me. Therefore, I speak to the mountain of debt in my life and command it to be gone. No matter how big the mountain of debt is, it's not bigger than my God.

I speak to all my debt and I command it to be paid. Debts, I'm talking to you and telling you to be paid in Jesus' name. Debts, be reduced and eliminated. I call my mortgage paid in Jesus' name. I call my vehicles paid off in Jesus' name. I call every loan and credit card paid off in Jesus' name. My God can bring water out of a rock, and He can feed thousands with a few pieces of fish and bread. My God can surely take care of my bills.

I declare that my God meets all my needs; therefore, all my bills are paid on time. I refuse to worry or have any anxious thought about my finances. I don't have to figure out where the money is coming from because that's God's concern. I have released my faith. Now I shall receive my provision.

Scriptures

If ye have faith as a grain of mustard seed, ye shall say unto this mountain, Remove hence to yonder place; and it shall remove; and nothing shall be impossible unto you.

Matthew 17:20

They thirsted not when he led them through the deserts: he caused the waters to flow out of the rock for them: he clave the rock also, and the waters gushed out.

Isaiah 48:21

But my God shall supply all your need according to his riches in glory by Christ Jesus.

Philippians 4:19

End the Day With God

The peace of God places garrisons around me. His peace gives me strength, comfort, and rest from all the events, circumstances, and challenges of this life. I will not carry the burden of my financial difficulties. Instead, I will cast all my care on Him. I will not worry or be anxious about anything. I will not let my mind or heart become troubled. Jesus will never leave me or forsake me. No weapon formed against me shall prosper. If God be for me, then surely no one can be against me.

God is working on my behalf. All of my debts are being eliminated and paid off. All my bills are paid on time. If my income is not enough to cover all my expenses, then God will make up the difference. God has promised to give His beloved sweet sleep, and I am His beloved, so that means me. I will sleep soundly and peacefully throughout the whole night. I will wake refreshed and encouraged and full of joy, ready to face a new day.

Scriptures

God's peace [shall be yours, that tranquil state of a soul assured of its salvation through Christ, and so fearing nothing from God and being content with its earthly lot of whatever sort that is, that peace] which transcends all understanding shall garrison mount guard over your hearts and minds in Christ Jesus.

Philippians 4:7 AMP

No weapon that is formed against thee shall prosper.

Isaiah 54:17

Peace I leave with you, my peace I give unto you; not as the world giveth, give I unto you. Let not your heart be troubled, neither let it be afraid.

John 14:27

When thou liest down, thou shalt not be afraid; yea, thou shalt lie down, and thy sleep shall be sweet.

Proverbs 3:24

PRAYER OF SALVATION

God loves you—no matter who you are, no matter what your past. God loves you so much that He gave His one and only begotten Son for you. The Bible tells us that "...whoever believes in him shall not perish but have eternal life" (John 3:16 NIV). Jesus laid down His life and rose again so that we could spend eternity with Him in heaven and experience His absolute best on earth. If you would like to receive Jesus into your life, say the following prayer out loud and mean it from your heart:

Heavenly Father, I come to You admitting that I am a sinner. Right now, I choose to turn away from sin, and I ask You to cleanse me of all unrighteousness. I believe that Your Son, Jesus, died on the cross to take away my sins. I also believe that He rose again from the dead so that I might be forgiven of my sins and made righteous through faith in Him. I call upon the name of Jesus Christ to be the Savior and Lord of my life. Jesus, I choose to follow You and ask that You fill me with the power of the Holy Spirit. I declare that right now I am a child of God. I am free from sin and full of the righteousness of God. I am saved in Jesus' name. Amen.

If you prayed this prayer to receive Jesus Christ as your Savior for the first time, please contact us on the Web at **www.harrisonhouse.com** to receive a free book.

Or you may write to us at
Harrison House
P.O. Box 35035 • Tulsa, Oklahoma 74153

Receive Healing Now!

A Beautiful Gift Edition to Set Life's Course for Victory!

ISBN-13:
978-1-57794-916-9

God has given powerful promises in His Word—peace, joy, health, provision, and more. Let these promises become reality for you, a friend, or a loved one by agreeing with God's Word!

The *Scripture Confessions Gift Collection* includes five books complete in one volume: *Victorious Living, Healing, Finances, for Moms,* and *for Dads*. This life-changing gift in beautiful Italian leather is a convenient and powerful Scripture resource designed to bring God's Word into busy lifestyles.

Available at fine bookstores
everywhere or visit
www.harrisonhouse.com.

Fast. Easy.
Convenient.

For the latest Harrison House product infor-
mation and author news, look no further
than your computer. All the details on our
powerful, life-changing products are just a
click away. New releases, E-mail
subscriptions, Podcasts, testimonies,
monthly specials—find it all in one place.
Visit harrisonhouse.com today!

harrisonhouse